Happy Kids,

Growing Biz

Publisher: Never Alone Coaching

Cover Design: Dalim

Printed by CreateSpace, an Amazon.com company

ISBN: 978-1534958654

www.NeverAloneCoaching.com

Happy Kids, Growing Biz

How I took a side business

to 6 figures while homeschooling 4 kids

By

Jen Hickle

About the Author

Jen Hickle is a fast-moving, passionate and driven business owner. In 1996 she started a small side company that allowed her to graduate from college debt-free. She took this business to 6 figures by strategically studying systems and marketing. Now she and her husband, Chris, work from home and help other business owners grow their companies! When not homeschooling or driving her kids to activities, Jen loves coffee, reading books, writing, traveling and having good conversation with friends while eating out!

Jen has won multiple awards for business excellence, social media marketing and a national Music School of the Year award. She has started 3 successful businesses. She and her family live in Minnesota.

INTRODUCTION

Here's to all the mamas balancing business, meal planning, carpools, play dates, birthday parties, laundry, cleaning, hiring, firing, marketing, editing the website, writing the copy, meetings, cleaning out the fridge, filling up the van, remembering birthdays, planning parties, running staff meetings, and dispensing medicine to kids and hubby.

To all the women fighting for their dreams while juggling all the daily tasks and chores. To the women who cry when no one is looking and don't get a haircut nearly often enough.

To the women who have fought to get here but still don't feel like they've even begun to fight.

To all the women who know the days are long but the years are short.

To you. To me. Cheers.

CHAPTER 1

The Journey

"Success seems to be largely a matter of hanging on after others have let go."
-William Feather

In 2003, I had a 2-year-old, an infant, and a husband in the hospital with a ruptured appendix. While he was recovering from an internal infection explosion and spending a week in the hospital, I was busy taking care of my babies and running back and forth to the hospital. Getting the mail, and taking over paying the bills, I found credit card statements that I did not know we had. I discovered we were $20,000 in debt from credit cards alone.

The world stopped that day.

I looked around at our brand new townhome that we had just built and a brand new SUV that we had just purchased and I realized the very, very deep pit we had dug for ourselves. Soon after my husband was home from the hospital and the weight of our situation settled on me, I lay in bed feeling trapped, confused, angry, and alone. I imagined grabbing my two young boys out of their cribs and leaving my husband. How did we get here? How did this happen? What does our future hold?

I didn't leave. Instead, we declared that it was our turning point. We made the hard decision to sell our car and our brand new, beautiful house. We worked very hard and deliberately over the next five years to get out of debt. The budget was sliced and diced until it felt like nothing was left. It was time to stop ignoring the budget, the numbers, and the mess. We had to tackle this head-on.

I bought food that would stretch as far as possible, using recipes with the word "frugal" in the title. One day in the grocery store, an older gentleman saw me using a calculator as I placed each item in the cart. Every decision mattered, and he could tell. Very gently, he pointed out the discount bin in the meat section—the meat was set to expire in a day or two, and deeply discounted in price. I stocked my freezer each week from that bin, and we filled in the gaps with pasta and rice. I cut coupons for everything, and drove to several stores each week, just to find the best deal for milk and toothpaste. I vowed not to purchase anything without a coupon. I treated myself to a gourmet coffee only on Tuesdays, when the mochas were discounted to $2.00. In the drive-through window, I handed the barista my assorted change, embarrassed that it came from crevices in my couch and the change drawer in my minivan.

In the summer, I only shopped at garage sales, and even then, my husband begrudgingly handed over a limited amount of cash and change for me to use. (I think my mother-in-law saw our predicament—because she offered to buy the kids shoes every year. What a blessing!)

The entire time that we clawed our way out of debt and attempted to re-wire our brains and lifestyle, I was growing my small business. The motivation to make more money to support our family was overwhelming. I did what I knew how to do, and I relied on books, friends and other business owners to fill in the gaps. I was desperate to make my little company grow.

At that time, I taught piano lessons and I hired other piano teachers to teach lessons as well. To make more money, I knew I had to multiply myself. I handled all the billing, scheduling, and administration. People called me for lessons, and I matched them with a teacher who would come to their home for lessons.

I worked every afternoon, while my kids napped, working on developing new systems and new organizational tools for my staff. I wrote emails and newsletters late at night, when my kids were finally asleep. I kept the business books I wanted to read on the back of the toilet and read a few pages in the bathroom every day. I took walks with the stroller and the tricycles, and then prayed for wisdom, direction, and ideas. I had a separate cell phone for the business, but because I was so busy with the kids, it sat in the drawer until I could answer the calls while my husband gave the kids a bath at night. I was so embarrassed to make follow up calls at 8:00pm, but my prospective clients were grateful that I had gotten back to them. I was good at what

I did and I closed nearly every sale, steadily adding new clients and growing my business.

During this whole time, we were also church planting. My husband was a youth pastor and then, an associate pastor, and because the churches were brand new, they couldn't afford to pay very much. I desperately wanted to grow my business to supplement our small ministry income.

One of the darkest days of this journey was when my husband switched from one church to another and the new church couldn't pay him at all. He has amazing techy skills, so he was hired right away as the computer guy at a fairly large company. However, with the commute in traffic every day, he was gone from 7:45am to 6:30pm. He would arrive home exhausted, and collapse on the couch. As he lay on the couch, and the kids begged him to play, my eyes would shoot daggers at him as I finished prepping for dinner. I had been home all day with a new baby, a 3-year old, a 5-year old, and a 7-year old and I wanted to collapse on the couch, too. He was exhausted and I was exhausted. I wondered whether or not our marriage would make it, or whether we could even survive that season. I constantly found myself in tears every day as I tried to do tasks that I wished he were at home to do for me such as to assemble the bike rack on the back of the van, kill the spider in the basement, shoo the bee out of my kitchen, change light bulbs, and replace water filters.

Daily, I would think: **"This is not what I signed up for. This is not what I wanted to do with my life."**

I knew that the job of a mom was important and I wanted to be with my kids. But I also wanted to work and make more money for our family. I would stare longingly at my computer and count down the hours until the kids were napping or having screen time so I could work on my business.

Over and over again, I thought: "If I could just make more money...if I could just grow my company...if I could just work harder...then things could change. If only I could enroll more students in my lessons and classes...if only I could figure out this marketing stuff."

I read every book I could find. I scoured the internet. I talked to anyone who would listen to me at the park while my kids played. I tried so hard.

In 2008, my dad was laid-off and suddenly the problem was bigger than just my small family and me. I saw my parents suffer and panic. I had to do something. Around my dining room table, we brainstormed, and together we launched a theatre company. They had been teaching music and theatre for years, I had been running the administrative side of my music lessons business, and together I knew we could form a powerful partnership. But now, I really had skin in the game. I was absolutely desperate to learn more practical skills for my business so I could make more money for myself and my parents. I dreamed of my husband being able to quit his job and work with me on my company so we could church plant without needing a salary from the ministry.

One day, while searching for answers online, I found a business coaching program, describing the answers exactly as what I was looking for. The price tag was absolutely shocking, so I quietly shut my computer and didn't tell my husband for a couple months. I thought about it constantly and prayed desperately and fervently. How would I come up with the money for this program? But how could I say "no" to the very answers I was so desperately seeking? I knew that taking this step would catapult me to the next level. I knew I had to figure out how to say "yes" to this opportunity.

When I finally got up the nerve to spill my secret to Chris, he was quiet. Finally, he looked at me steadily. "We can do this. We'll figure out a way." I was shocked. We had JUST climbed out of debt. I didn't think there was any way we could swing the cost of this program. We couldn't go backwards into debt. But my very frugal, very conservative, safe husband said, "We have to do this. We have to get answers. This isn't debt—it's an investment."

This coaching program wasn't just a purchase—it was a trip to a conference. We had to buy plane tickets and reserve a hotel room, plus pay for the coaching program. I thought I was going to be sick. But as I sat in that gigantic conference room, pen scribbling furiously with all the notes I was taking, I *knew* we had made the right decision. All the questions, all the gaps in my knowledge, all the wonderings vanished. Here I had found answers. Here I had found help. I had found hope!

Fast-forward 5 years. My husband was able to quit his job—because our music school grew more than enough to replace his salary. We have a commercial location, three employees working at our front desk (I don't even answer the phones anymore,) and we have 30 teachers who work for us and teach over 400 students at our studio each week. Our lessons and classes grew, like I prayed! In fact, we had to knock down walls and build more rooms for more lessons!

My parents' theatre company grew so much that they spun off with a different name. We share students and marketing, but we are two distinctive companies now; both are thriving and growing!

I don't have to shop in the discounted bin of meat anymore. In fact, I order groceries online and they are delivered to my doorstep. Just the other day, I visited my old coffee shop where I used to hand over my fistful of change. This time, I had $100 cash in my purse. I started to get tears in my eyes. How things have changed in only a couple of years!

We have NO credit card debt, we travel at least 3 times a year, and we enjoy the freedom of working and schooling from home. We have been to Washington, D.C., North and

South Carolina, Texas, California, and Arizona in the last two years. We travel because we love it. We love showing our kids different cultures and giving them experiences that they will remember forever. The money we invested in the coaching program was quickly recuperated as my business immediately started growing and thriving with the answers that I had been seeking. We've continued to invest thousands of dollars in classes, coaching and conferences. Never once have we regretted our purchase.

As our business has grown and been streamlined, one of the most important things we've gained is *time wealth*. As we have worked through a very specific, deliberate process to re-define what we want for our life, eliminate time wasters, and automate processes in our business, we have fallen in love with life again. We have time to spend with our kids, have friends over for dinner and deep discussions, and time to help other business owners. We love helping and serving at our third church plant (without having to ask for a salary!), and raising and homeschooling our kids.

The number one question that people ask me is "How do you do it all?" My answer is found in the acronym "REAL."

Re-define where you are going
Eliminate time wasters
Automate everything you can
Love what you do and do what you love

This formula has transformed my life and now I'm focused on helping others change their life, too! Together, Chris and I help business owners take the important, proven steps to improving their lives and their businesses. I've done it for myself, and I've also helped many others achieve the same results! It's hard work, it's intentional, and it's not overnight. But the results are worth it! Your family and your business need you to make this change. And I'm going to show you how.

CHAPTER 2

Re-define where you are going.

"Goals in writing are dreams with deadlines."
-Brian Tracy

I have a vision board on my wall. I have pictures of places I want to travel, goals I want to accomplish, and words that inspire me. I change my board about once a year, after I accomplish my goals.

It is absolutely imperative [of vital importance; crucial] that you have vision for where you are headed. Set your eyes on the goal and head in that direction. The path will not be a straight line. You'll have obstacles and setbacks. But you must know where you are headed before you start walking.

When I had my second baby, my best friend and I decided to attend a Bible Study that was offered through our church. It was after dark, my 3-month-old baby was in the backseat, and we were trying to find this house. My friend exclaimed, "I know where it is! It's on the other side of that lake! But how do we get there?"

Goals may seem just in front of us, but finding the road that leads us there can be a challenge. You have to take the journey one step at a time and just do the next thing in front of you. I'm a visionary and an activator—I love to take action. I don't like inactivity and I don't like to wait. But I have to continually remind myself that my vision is slightly disconnected to my next right step. I don't get to take 3 giant steps to reach my goal. No, it's more like 2,000 baby steps to reach the goal.

Keep your eyes on your goal, but also break down the steps into the next right thing.

You must continually re-define where you are headed, especially as a mom business owner. Having babies and kids in the house changes everything. The goal that you were once walking towards may need to be modified or changed. You will constantly need to re-work the plan. And that's okay.

During the last 15 years, I've had to adjust how I work and where I work as the stages of my kids and my business have changed. I am continually re-evaluating what is working and what isn't, and making the necessary changes. I have my eyes on my goals ahead and I ruthlessly pursue them.

I had to chuckle recently when a friend asked me, "How do you work from home? Don't you get distracted?"

Of course I do! But here's how I deal with it. When working at home, I have found that it's important to have a "home base." This could be a desk or space where you keep your computer, calendar and office supplies. Secondly, it's important to have a work bag where you can quickly pack up and head to the library, coffee shop, or outside. Working from home means freedom and flexibility, so make sure you can change locations when needed! That's one of the best perks!

Strategically pick a work environment for your home base.
Do you need to be near small children? Away from
teenagers? At the dining room to collaborate with a
spouse? Or at a desk so you can't see all the household
chores pulling at you? The location of where you work will
largely define your productivity. But first, you must assess
your needs. Not everyone can work in a home "office" and
not everyone can work at the kitchen table. Some need to
be near a window to think and create, and some are
distracted by seeing outside. Be willing to move around
and be flexible, until you find what is best.

I have discovered that being at home has great rewards
because I don't have to rush out the door every morning,
gulping down my coffee. If I wake up early, I can get some
research and writing done while the whole house sleeps.
When the kids are eating breakfast, I do my morning
routine (shower, get dressed, make bed, do hair, do
makeup.) Afterwards, I get straight back to work or start
my kids on their homeschooling projects and assignments.
I ignore the kitchen, laundry, and floors. I barrel through
as many tasks and projects as possible until lunchtime.
During a lunch break, I assess the condition of the house,
have kids clean up their art and cooking messes, load the

dishwasher, eat, etc. After lunch, I'll slow down my pace a little bit, finish what I'm working on, and transition into "mom mode" where I am driving kids to theatre, dance, friends' houses, etc. Some afternoons, while they are in activities, I'll settle into a comfortable booth at the library where I can really get a lot of writing and research done in pure silence.

When I'm stuck and can't solve a problem, the nice thing about working from home is using household chores as a distraction and thinking tool. I've hashed out many dilemmas in my mind while elbow-deep in sudsy water, washing dishes. Folding laundry isn't a chore—it's therapeutic—compared to dealing with that difficult customer or hard employee situation.

When the weather is gorgeous and pleasant, I love sitting outside on the deck while working! Having trees and nature around me, and hearing my kids play nearby makes me appreciative of the life we have built.

For staff meetings, I head into my studio to meet with my employees, or we use a free conference line. Everyone dials in, and we can be done in less than 20 minutes. It's fast and efficient, and we can all call from wherever we are. Once a month, we meet face to face at the studio and can have a little more time building camaraderie and relationships.

My iPhone is my best work-at-home tool. I can be on the go, on vacation, running errands, or on the couch, and from my smartphone, I can answer emails, access my online notes, see my studio's schedule, and view the security cameras at my studio location. I am on-call for any emergency any time, but I know everything is okay when I have my phone in my hand.

I also have an Apple Watch, which I LOVE because I can glance down and see the date, the current outside temp, my next upcoming appointment, and, of course, the time. A slight buzz on my wrist tells me when I have a notification. I can glance down and see if it's important or if it can wait, without having to look at my phone and get pulled away from what I am doing.

To be productive, some people are motivated by outside forces, some from within. Some are rebellious and want to do things their own way. I am extremely motivated from within, and I like to create structure and discipline. Therefore, working from home is the perfect situation for me. It's not easy—but it works, and I love it. I plan on being interrupted by my kids dozens of times a day. It's just a fact. However, because some projects require "no interrupting," I have always made it a priority to get out of the house to work at a coffee shop or library at least one day per week. I also will often hire a nanny or mother's helper to come to my house one or two days a week, just to play with the kids, clean up the kitchen, wash a few dishes, and be the Director of Fun Activities. I feel less mom-guilt while working when I hear giggles from Uno and The Game of Life coming from the other room.

Working at home has vastly changed and evolved in the last 15 years. The most stressful part of working from home with my husband, while homeschooling my kids, is how messy the house gets. It's very distracting and can ruin my mood quickly. So, I hire a house cleaner to come every Friday for 3 hours. It's a life-saver. Once the house is cleaned and picked up, I can think clearly again! It's a gift and a necessity for a family who works at home and schools at home.

Every semester I reevaluate what is working and what isn't. I write out the entire week's schedule and make adjustments where needed. It's a continual work in progress and I am willing to make changes when things aren't working. I also must create and sustain boundaries that I have set in place. When I've blocked off time to work, I can't say 'yes' when a friend needs a listening ear or help with her kids during that time. I want to be loving and giving with my time, but not if it means rushing around all the time. I believe in building in margin, so there is time for emergencies, extended family, and friends. But if you are the one creating your schedule, you are the only one who can keep it. And sometimes, that means saying 'no' gently and firmly.

For mothers of small children: ALWAYS hire help. If you are working, you are making money. You must invest some of that money back into yourself, and that means hiring a babysitter at least once a week. Then, hire a house cleaner. Start with every other week. Do what you can with what resources you have. There's no way you can run yourself ragged and be successful at your work. And even if you are successful, if you've lost all joy and peace in your life, it's not worth it.

Be sure to schedule regular dates with your spouse, and keep those dates! Now that my kids are old enough to be home alone, my husband and I go out to lunch and to the chiropractor every week. I love those times together and our marriage needs it.

I also go out to dinner with my best friend every Monday night. It's something we have done for 14 years! And we both love Mondays because of it! It's a chance in our week to step away from life, analyze, discuss, share, encourage, and uplift each other. My husband can't provide everything I need emotionally, and having a close friendship that I can lean on is absolutely necessary. I have other friends who check in with me during the week via text or Facebook messenger. It's important to have people in your life who understand what you're doing and can encourage you and celebrate with you! In fact, having a solid support system is one of the most important things you need to work from home. Surround yourself with people who "get" you and celebrate you. Your life and your business depend on your sanity!

Download the workbook companion for this book at www.neveralonecoaching.com. Together, we'll breakdown your schedule and goals.

If I have learned one thing for sure, it's that life is always changing and shifting. Just when I think I've gotten comfortable, things change again. Especially with kids in the house—their needs and schedules are always in flux. This is incredibly challenging for a business owner! Just when we establish a work schedule, everything is uprooted and we have to start from square one again!

When I was pregnant, my whole outlook on life changed. Everything went sort of black and white for me. I didn't have the same energy as I normally do, and with my fourth baby, I struggled with anxiety every day. Just starting a load of laundry gave me an anxiety attack, so running my business was incredibly difficult. Instead of marketing, I wanted to hibernate. Every pregnancy gave me morning sickness for the first 12 weeks. And I'm not talking about "Oh, I feel a little nauseous." No, I threw up every day for 12 weeks (mostly in the morning, but sometimes in the kitchen sink as I attempted to make my kids lunch.) Every time, I knew I was pregnant before I even took a pregnancy test because of all the puking. I lost twenty pounds with every pregnancy in the first trimester because all I could eat was fruit slushes and crackers. I also had to take a nap every single day. So much for working during naptime! I would bribe, pray, plead, and cajole my kids into taking a nap so I could crawl into bed.

When I was pregnant with baby number 3, I would put the 18-month-old down for a nap in his crib, and then bring the 3-year-old into my bed, snuggle with him and rub his back, silently pleading for him to just fall asleep so I could sleep.

When I wasn't pregnant, nap time was a great time to catch up on emails and get work done, but when pregnant, all bets were off. All I craved was sleep.

As my kids got older, and naptime became a thing of the past, I grieved losing that time of silence. Even though I liked the freedom of not being bound by set nap times so we could be out and about more, I wondered how on earth I would ever get any work done. So I had to re-evaluate everything once again. I learned to work on my computer with cartoons in the background. "Screen time" after lunch became my sanity saver. I would also return phone calls and emails on the deck while my kids played in the yard and in the sandbox. I became a Master Jedi in sneaking in work whenever I could.

Now that my kids are even older, it's a different kind of hard. I can work in my office and they don't have to be supervised 24/7, but they have complicated schedules and constantly need to be driven to one activity or another. Or, they have a personal crisis and need to talk. I have to drop everything and turn into a counselor and problem-solver. My older kids don't go to bed at 7:00 or 8:00pm anymore. I used to be able to count on a couple hours of work time after the kids were in bed. Now my kids aren't even home from activities until 9:30 or 10:00pm! Many moms like to work late at night, while their kids are sleeping, but I am a morning person (my kids trained me to wake up at 6am for years!), and I would rather work early in the morning when I'm rested and refreshed. Bottom line: do what works best for you!

No matter what stage of life you're in, I bet you feel like it's constantly changing, too. The best piece of advice I've ever received is to just accept that nothing will ever stay the same. Things will always change, and we have to make peace with it.

One sanity saver that I've found is to make a weekly schedule and completely re-evaluate and change it every January, May, and September. It seems like many of my kids' activities are semester-based, so I can always ask myself, "What's working? What's not?" and make the necessary changes in our schedule. Items that always get budgeted into our schedule are:

- Weekly dates with my husband
- Weekly chiropractor visits
- Regular family dinner times
- Grocery day
- Church
- Laundry day
- Work day OUT of the house (somewhere quiet!)
- Dinner with my best friend

I prioritize these big rocks into our schedule because they are sanity savers. Have you heard about the big rock illustration? Basically, if I gave you a jar, 7 big rocks, 15 small rocks, and a cup of sand, and told you to fit them all into the jar, you would need to start with the big rocks. The small rocks and the sand can fit into the crevices, but if you don't get those big rocks in first, they'll never fit later.

Decide what your big rocks are (family, spouse, work, etc.,) and get those in your schedule first!

Continually re-evaluate your schedule and make small changes. You don't have to overhaul everything. Start with small changes that are attainable. But be bold with your boundaries. When you work from home or own your own business, you are the only one that can hold your boundaries in place. So be firm and loving, and say 'no' when you have to.

Recently, we took a family vacation to Arizona. Every morning, I woke up early before anyone else to journal, think, and pray. While I was away from "normal" life, I was able to process so many things about our schedule and our routines.

I asked myself:
What can I change?
What can I adjust?

How can I go back home with renewed vision for my life, my kids, and my business?

I know I can't change the past. But I can change course and affect the future.

On vacation, I like to read powerful, transformational books. When I am relaxed, my mind is open to new concepts and I'm more receptive to change.

I also fill many pages in my journal as I process all these important findings. I find it so healing and therapeutic to actually write down my thoughts as I think them. It helps

me sort things out and I have a recording of that process, too.

I also love to listen to new-to-me music albums. Whenever I do this, I stamp the images of vacation on top of the music and anytime I listen to that music, I am transported back to the sights and smells of vacation. It's amazing and powerful!

It's vitally important to step away from normal life, responsibilities and obligations to reassess what you love and appreciate your life, and also ask yourself, "What can I change?" Honestly, I think we all need to do this more often. If you can't get a vacation, ask your husband or mother or a friend to take your kids for an entire day. Go to a new town or just drive. Take a walk around a lake. Step away from life so you can really think, process, and plan. Some of my homeschooling friends get a hotel room overnight and write their semester lesson plans, away from the distractions at home.

Taking time to re-define where you're headed and what you want from life is incredibly powerful. You can work through more issues and problems by stepping away than you could ever do while sitting at your desk at home.

Sometimes you just need a different perspective to see your life clearly.

Also, you need to assess where your business is headed. Is it in trouble? Are you headed down the wrong road or worse still, stalled on the side of the road?

Several years ago, I was headed to a fun swimming day with my four kids strapped into car seats, when I heard a strange sound. I immediately turned off the blaring kid music and with dread, realized my tire blew out. I frantically pulled off to the side of the road while traffic continued to whizz by me on my left. On my right, there was a sharp incline—literally, the shoulder of the road ended and a sharp cliff dropped down to a ravine below. I have NEVER prayed so desperately for help. I was terrified, and yet I had to act upbeat and confident so I wouldn't panic the little passengers in my van.

"It's going to be okay," I said in a high-pitched, sing-songy voice. "We are going to be JUST fine!" I promised with false bravado. My hands were shaking, but I had to keep smiling, keep nodding, and KEEP THEM CALM. All the while, I am glancing desperately out my window, hoping nothing will hit us, hoping help was on the way. I called my husband to come help, but he was stuck at work, over 45 minutes away. I dialed my brother in law, and thankfully, he was home and could come to my rescue.

I have never been so happy to see anyone, before or since, when he pulled up behind me to change my tire. "Thank you! Thank you for coming!" I exclaimed.

I'll never forget his response: "Of course. That's what I'm here for!"

His calm voice and assurance literally still brings tears to my eyes every time I pass that spot on the freeway.

He came to my rescue. He had the tools and the knowledge to fix my flat tire. He was calm and steady, and he got it done. We were safe and our tire was fixed.

A couple years later, I experienced a different kind of car trouble. It was during a particularly hot summer. Every few days, I would hear a horrible flapping noise coming from the front of my minivan. The weird thing was that it would only happen occasionally. And of course, it would never be when my husband, Chris, was with me! So naturally, he thought I was hearing things (or crazy).

One particularly hot summer day, I was leaving my music studio and the noise was so awful and horrible that I drove immediately to the nearest auto shop because I thought we were all *going to die.* I'm sure I looked like the typical frantic-crazy-woman: "There's something wrong with my van! It's horrible! I don't want to stall with 4 kids in the car again! You have to look!" The guy sighed patiently, attempted to calm me down, and then told me to drive up on those strange wedge blocks so he could look under the engine. I was so scattered and scared that I couldn't do it. I got out and made him drive up the ramp.

After looking under the van and in the engine, he declared. "There's nothing wrong."

"What? But there is a horrible flapping sound! You HAVE to find something wrong! I can't drive this thing!"

I drove away despondent. I KNEW something was wrong, and yet no one could find anything. I wracked my brain, listened to that stupid flapping noise, and then inspiration hit! Maybe the sound was coming from the ROOF of the van! As soon as I was home, I climbed onto the side of the van, and looked at the luggage rack. Nothing.

Then I saw it. The source of the flapping: the rubber that encased my windshield glass was loose! The hotter the sun, the more the rubber loosened and flapped in the wind, and especially when I drove at high speeds!

I was elated! I knew there was a problem, I identified it, and now I could get it fixed!

Did I have the tools or the knowledge of HOW to fix it? No. But I could call the glass company and THEY knew what to do!

It's the same in your business.

You may have the knowledge that *something* isn't working right, or you may have *panic* that something is seriously wrong. You may have even identified WHAT is wrong. But now, you need the tools and know-how, so you can get it fixed.

Car trouble always brings a sense of dread. The cost! The bills! What will they find? Sometimes I cling to false hope: Maybe the problem will just go away? Unfortunately, in most cases, when I've ignored a transmission problem or delayed my oil changes, I've only made the problem worse.

Are you bravely putting on a smiling face, keeping everyone calm around you, but inwardly panicking about all the danger around you? It could be a small problem, like a flat tire, but if you stay stranded, it could turn into a much worse situation.

Or, your "flapping noise" could be a perceived HUGE, HORRIBLE problem, when it can actually be fixed with something very simple.

You are the driver in your life and in your business. You know where you're going. But you may need an expert to help diagnose and fix the problems you are facing.

I don't know much about cars. But when the engine in my van starts making strange noises, I bring it into the shop. I don't pop the hood and start tinkering around on my own—I have no idea how all those parts work together. Sure, I could look up videos on YouTube, but I don't want to even learn about the complexities of my car engine. And I certainly don't want to make the problem worse. But I can bring it to someone who does, and who can help me. I need my vehicle working properly so it will *get me where I'm going.*

If you're suspecting that your business may be in trouble, here's what to do:

1. **Stop Ignoring the Warning Signs**. It's time to "pop the hood" of your business and do an engine check. You may need a new transmission or you just may need an oil change, but you need to find out. Talk to someone you can trust and get their honest feedback. A business coach is someone who has walked the same road you are on and has helped many other business owners. They can give you tangible help and help assess what's going on and how you can fix the problem.

2. **Get help.** It may be time to hire someone and expand your team to get you out of this rough spot. The focus you are placing on your problems is wasting more time and money than taking the time to hire a new employee, a virtual assistant (VA) or a service to help you. Don't automatically say: "We can't afford it." Sometimes you can't afford *not to*. Take time to

evaluate: Will your new employee actually make your company more money because of the business they will generate? Or, can you make more money if the new employee takes over the non-income producing tasks that are taking up so much of your time? Building your team can get you out of this rut, and up and over the hump to the next level.

3. **Invest in resources.** Pushing through for a season is sometimes required, but it may be time to spend some money to take this huge load off your shoulders. If you're always thinking: "There's got to be a better way," there probably is. There are endless software choices that can streamline many of the tasks that you are still doing the hard way. When I have researched and found CRM tools (Customer Relationship Management) for my companies, it has freed up so much time and released me from so much stress and anxiety! If you're still using paper or spreadsheets or Excel to track customer information, orders, or enrollment information, it's time to upgrade to new tools. If you aren't regularly communicating with your current or former clients, you need a system to easily market your business. Having the right tools can make all the

difference, so make sure your tools are the best for your business.

4. **Seek Support.** Share your struggles with like-minded friends and get their input and feedback. Like-minded Facebook groups have been some of my favorite resources for support and help. You shouldn't suffer alone—find people who understand what you're going through and can offer support or practical tools when you're down. You don't have to do this all alone. Help could be just around the corner!

5. **Get perspective.** I'm really dramatic. (My parents are theatre directors. Enough said.) So I often wail, "I'm FAILING!" My extremely logical husband informs me that you need less than 60% to FAIL, so I'm probably getting a B or a C. Well, honestly, I hate anything less than an A (that's my perfectionism speaking,) but it's impossible to be perfect at everything. Sometimes you have to be happy with imperfect action or with just "good enough." Maybe your business isn't in trouble, but you need perspective to see where you really are and where you are going.

6. **Shape a positive attitude**. Most people climb into
   bed and review everything they said throughout the
   day, and how they should have said it better. Or, they
   think of everything they still need to get done. I
   challenge you to instead, every night, before bed, name
   3 things you are thankful for or 3 things that went
   WELL that day. Focusing on the positive will
   completely change your outlook and your attitude.
   When you stay in gratitude, you will avoid spiraling
   down into depression or self-hatred. I have a sign on
   my wall that says: "There is always, always, always
   something to be grateful for." It's true.

As you shape your vision and re-define your goals,
remember the most important point is just to have a vision
for where you are going. It may be fuzzy and it may be
vague, but keep faith and trust in what the future could
look like.

I'm not a huge advocate for detailed business plans (I think
too many things change along the journey.) But the most
important step you can take is creating a vision board:
print pictures of your dream house, your dream vacation,
the number you want your income to grow to, the number

of clients you want to serve, and whatever else inspires and motivates you. Create it and put it on your wall where you'll see it every day. It will remind you where you are going and why you are on this journey.

CHAPTER 3

Eliminate time-wasters

"If you want something you've never had, you must be willing to do what you've never done!"
-Thomas Jefferson

1. Eliminate the mental clutter

Are you feeling stuck? Are your wheels spinning, as if you just can't get forward traction?

Everywhere you look, there are dishes to be washed, clothes to be folded, calls to return, library books collecting fines. And yet, what you really need to do is get to your computer, answer emails, book new clients, and make more money.

The pressure is all around you. You want to be a good mama, wife, friend, and daughter. You want to say "yes" to everyone who needs your help. There's just not enough of YOU to go around.

It's not easy keeping so many balls juggling in the air. You probably feel discouraged and let down. Maybe you even feel like a failure. The truth is: you're not. Instead of focusing on everything you have to do, make a list of what you've accomplished! Think of the tears you've wiped away, the friend you encouraged yesterday, the project you finished last week. Think of your son or daughter and the beautiful person they are becoming. Think of everything you've done this year so far! Clear your mind of the mental clutter that is screaming at you.

As a high achiever, I wake up each day to a clean slate. I'm not even thinking about my accomplishments from yesterday or earlier in the year. I've won multiple awards for excellence in business, a social media marketing award, and a national Music School of the Year contest, and yet I tend to forget everything that I've accomplished and I just keep pushing forward. I've literally had to create a list of my accomplishments and keep it near my journal so I can remember how far I've come. You need to do the same thing. Literally, make a list of what you have overcome and what you have achieved! We can't always keep pushing, pushing, pushing. We need to take the time to celebrate our success.

Stop yelling at yourself, and instead, speak to yourself the way you would speak to your friend. It sounds strange, but when the voices in my head start saying, "What is your problem? This house is a disaster! The lawn is a mess!" I actually think to myself, "That's not very nice way to talk to me." Then I say soothingly, "Jen, you are doing such a good job. I see how hard you are trying. Don't worry—we'll get that done tomorrow." I change the condescending voice in my head to the soothing voice of a friend. Make a conscious choice like this—it makes a huge difference.

2. Eliminate the endless task lists.

Are you feeling completely overwhelmed? You don't even know where to start? You don't know what's important or urgent or what you're forgetting?

Let's take a moment and do something together. Grab a brand new piece of paper (or my favorite—Post-it Notes with lines on them!) Write at the top: "To Do." Now start fresh. Make a list of everything you need to get done. Everything that is clamoring for your attention...everything that is screaming to be done... Consolidate all your crazy lists and pieces of scrap paper into one list. If you need more than one, continue on the next page but put the most important and urgent items on page one. When I'm realistic with myself, I can only accomplish one To-Do list per week. That's about 10 items. And that's because, for every item, there are probably 5 steps attached to that one task! To get out of a rut, you have to be realistic with what you can accomplish!

I also like to break down my To-Do lists into categories: Work, House, Kids. Home improvement goals are often important to me, but not urgent, so that Post-it Note lasts several months and can be pushed out and delayed when needed. My kids' To Do list is often urgent: someone needs new soccer cleats, dance shoes, or a birthday gift for a friend. I have notebooks of goals and big picture tasks for my business, but on the Post-it Note, I write down the tasks that need to be done this week. There are a million apps and tools that you can use for To Do lists, but I'm still a pen and paper gal. I need to see my lists and have them on my desk. If I organize all my tasks beautifully and shut my computer, then POOF they are gone and off to Netflix I go!

The bottom line is: do what works best for your personality. Don't use paper or an app because you think you "should." Use what actually works for your personality and learning style. And if you don't know, keep trying different methods! Figure out what works.

3. Eliminate the tasks that you can hire out.

Next, let's make a list of anything you can hire out. If your website still isn't finished, it's time to have someone else take it over and get it done fast. If bookkeeping is sucking the life right out of you, it's time to hire someone! If you're like me, you're probably a creative, right-brain person. Therefore, you shouldn't be doing your own books! Numbers scare me and while I like *earning* money, I don't like tracking it and I HATE receipts. That's why I pay a bookkeeper! I promise: you can't do it all. You need to hire someone to help you. Shut down the guilt and even shut out the voices saying, "I can't afford it." I promise—if you hire tasks done, you'll actually make MORE money because you'll be focusing on what you do best!

Please—I beg of you—open a separate business account. Do not use your personal bank account for business expenses. Do not use your business account to pay for dinner. Keep the accounts separate so you can truly see what you are earning, what you are paying yourself, and what your expenses are. If you seriously want to grow your business, you have to be serious about your bank accounts and your bookkeeping! Hire help. That's the best advice I can give to you!

4. Eliminate physical clutter

The last thing that helps me get out of a crazy stuck place is to turn on a timer and clean up the house for just 15 minutes. I yell "All hands on deck!" and all the kids help quickly straighten pillows and remotes, and unload/load the dishwasher. They straighten the shoes in the entryway and put away their schoolbooks, dance shoes, water bottles, etc. Just seeing a clean surface and fresh "canvas" helps me THINK straight again. Then I can get to my To-Do list and actually move forward.

One of the best things you can do for your sanity and for your business is to de-clutter. Purge. Give away and throw away. If you're just not an organizer, get the help of someone who is a sister, a friend, your daughter, or a professional organizer. If you're doing too much laundry all week, then have fewer clothes! My kids only own about 8 outfits each. Keep it simple! If you're homeschooling, get rid of the curriculum you aren't using. Throw away the guilt and the clutter! The less stuff you have to clean and organize, the more you will be able to think clearly. This isn't a one-time project. It's a mindset. I am continually thinking, "What do I need to give away? Throw away? How can I simplify?"

5. Eliminate the guilt

Homeschooling my kids is my #1 focus, but it's not full time. I talk to new homeschooling moms ALL the time that think homeschooling needs to look like school. It doesn't, and it can be done after a few hours in the morning. The reality is that more and more moms NEED to work part time just to put food on the table, or to help pay for co-ops and field trips, vacations, and other expenses. It <u>can</u> be part time and you <u>can</u> be okay with that!

(I would much rather work and pay for a math tutor for my kids. I like working and I don't like math! I stick to my strengths, make money, and I can pay the tutor who loves math! Love it!)

Not long ago, I was feeling guilty wherever I was. Guilty if I was home and not working. Guilty if I was working and not home. I finally asked myself: "Do you want to be frazzled 24/7 or do you want to be a good, happy Mama when you're with your kids?" So I made a decision to **be fully present wherever I am.**

Be 100% present, wherever you are—work, school, or play. When ideas pop into your head, just take notes on your phone so you can get back to it later. When you're playing a game with your kids, be fully engaged. When you're working, don't worry about home and continually text your husband or babysitter. Be focused and get your work done! Moms, I know it's hard! But the rewards are worth it if we focus on what's in front of us instead of spreading ourselves out in a million directions.

6. Embrace the season you are in!

When my kids were really little, I had to look at my dirty floors and tell them: YOU HAVE TO WAIT. I picked one day per week to clean the house and ignored the crumbs the rest of the time (or asked a kid to run the vacuum.) I purposefully avoid my kids' bedroom and the playroom, or I will find a million projects to do or start cleaning. The HARDEST thing for me is cluttered, dirty kitchen counters. So that is a priority for me. My kids take turns washing all the countertops after all the meals, and if it gets forgotten, I choose to not get angry but just quickly do it myself. Choose one priority for yourself and stick to it. But do NOT get sucked into cleaning all the time. It's just not an option when you own your own company or work from home. To have happy kids and a growing business, you have to choose what gets left undone, and you have to be at peace with it.

Now that they are older, my kids do the laundry, dishes, wash the counters, clean bathrooms, and vacuum. It's far from perfect because they are still in training, but I am so grateful that they are learning these skills. I am thrilled that my kids will have such vital life skills when they launch out of my home and into the world. Instead of feeling guilty that I am busy working, I am grateful that they are developing a sense of responsibility, character, and practical skills for their future. When I walk into the kitchen and see the crumbs by the toaster and the dishes stacked up in the sink, I can choose to be frustrated, or I can choose to sing the Frozen song, "Let it go!" and dance around the kitchen. It makes the kids laugh and it breaks the stress and tension! Sometimes you just have to do interpretive dance and make your family laugh. It's better than anger and we are making memories, people!

On Facebook recently, a blogger wrote: "Just keepin' it real!" and posted a picture of her family room. It was messy, filled with toys and unfolded laundry. She pointed out that too often we compare ourselves to perfection in the media and hold ourselves to much too high of a standard. We start believing that everyone is doing a better job than we are. Everyone agreed and started posting pictures of their messy living rooms in the comments. It was great. Then, in the midst of all this chaos was a picture of a perfectly clean family room and a mom who commented: "This is my living room. It's clean and perfect because my kids are gone. And I miss them. I miss the mess."

Tears welled up in my eyes. I don't want a quiet, empty, peaceful house yet. My kids are still growing and I want them under my roof. It is a joy and a privilege to raise children. I won't waste their childhood being frustrated about the mess. When my husband wails, "Why don't they put anything away?" I reply, "Because they are children." They are not mini-adults. They are kids. Kids who drop their music bag and run outside to play soccer. They are carefree and quickly on to the next task. Oh, that I could be so carefree and love life like that again! I want to soak up their energy and zest for life, and not despise the trail they leave behind. There is always time in the day to declare, "Room rescue!" And everyone pitches in to clean up and put books, gear, coats, and shoes away. Embrace the beautiful mess. Smile at your kids more often. Give them your love and attention and stop worrying about your house so much!

It's been said that you can choose two out of three: happy kids, clean house, or sanity. You can't have all three. I would agree. Yes, the days are super long and exhausting. But truly, the years are short. Soon, our kids will be gone. Let's enjoy them while we can.

CHAPTER 4

Automate Everything You Can

"Everyone is trying to accomplish something big, not realizing that life is made up of little things."
-Frank A. Clark

I used to think that if I automated everything in my business and my life, that all creativity would be sucked right out of my life. I am an organized person, but I love to be creative and free, and I was afraid that systems would become shackles and I would feel restricted.

Recently, my husband mentioned that we should systemize our marketing even more and I whined, "Don't take away the last trace of freedom from me! I *need* to be able to have inspiration and creativity hit me and just *go with it*." Since what we teach to others is systems and automation, he looked at me like I had three heads. "I'm not trying to take *anything* from you," he said. "I'm trying to take away more mental clutter so you don't have to think about these things anymore. Now you can write, create, and coach business owners *more*. You love those things, right? So let's systemize the marketing so you don't have to wait for creativity to hit to get it done!"

He made so much sense that I had to walk away. I hate when he's right!

Seriously, though—for creative business owners, we have the fear that automation will suck the life right out of us. It's simply not true. The more we can systematize and automate; the MORE creative we can be in the things that are truly enjoyable!

When my kids were young babies, I followed someone named "The Flylady." She sent out daily emails, coaching moms and wives how to organize and systematize their homes. Little by little, she brainwashed me. Some of the best tools I have today are from those years of her voice in my inbox every day. She insisted on assigning specific tasks to certain days of the week. Monday was for vacuuming the floors and Thursday was the day to pay bills and go through the paperwork. This has been my sanity keeper for years. If you want to work successfully from home, you have to establish routines for everything. You will simply lose your mind if you are in the middle of everything all the time. Choose a day to go grocery shopping (or better yet, order groceries online.) Choose a day to do ALL the laundry. Get it done and put away. (I know it's hard. But running a business is hard. We have to do hard things to get some sanity!)

Block off times in your week for working, interviewing new staff, staff meetings, and marketing, and then stick to the schedule! Yes, revamp it when it's not working. But first, set it and stick to it. You'll have to start new habits if you want to see changes in your life. You can complain about it, or you can fix it. It's your choice!

Now, what do you do when the unimaginable happens?

Cancer. Death. Accidents. Flooding. Sickness.

When unforeseen circumstances come out of nowhere like a punch to the gut, and you're left gasping for breath, how do you keep going? How do you run your business when all the adrenaline, energy, and excitement are gone?

When all you want to do is go crawl back in bed (or in a dark hole) and you're the leader, how do you react? What do you fall back on? The first thing I do is pray.

Sometimes ALL I can do is throw my hands up in surrender and ask God for help, peace, and guidance. He is faithful to take the wheel and drive for a while.

The second thing I do is lean back on my systems.

When grief has left me limp and lifeless, and I can barely get myself out of bed, I go back to what I set up for myself in times of energy and inspiration.

I look at my monthly marketing calendar: What am I supposed to be doing today? Even if I don't FEEL like it, I can start my newsletter, send my emails, update my website, and check our monthly profit and loss spreadsheet.

Even if I don't feel like CREATING or writing anything, I can do the mundane tasks because it doesn't take emotion to check off certain items on your To-do list.

If you only rely on creativity and emotion to move forward, grief and loss can sink your ship.

In the good times and in the light, map out the plan for your month (it should rotate every month) and for the week. What needs to always happen? What is predictable? For example, I send out a monthly newsletter, so every month I have to:

- Write my article

- Select pictures

- Gather data and statistics from the month

- Send to the printer

- Copy it to my website

- Email it to my list

- Post it on Facebook

Except for writing the main article, I can do the rest of those things without much creative juice flowing.

Here's a huge tip for you: Save your creative tasks for when you are feeling creative!

Don't waste your creative energy doing mundane things, if you can use that energy to CREATE. Likewise, if you're not "feeling" it, go back to your systems and do what you know needs to be done.

Delegate

I have many people around me, helping things to get accomplished every day of the week whether or not I "feel" like doing those things. My job is to manage and oversee those people, and even when I'm feeling less than 100%, these things get done, because I've trained them well. If I had not trained them and clearly explained what I expect, then when I'm down for the count, those things would fall down around me.

Instead, because they've clearly been taught the system, things can run "without" me for a while. Many of my business owners think that if their employees aren't a good fit, then they need to step back in. "This isn't working," they say. "It's better if I do it myself." No! Just because your employee isn't working out doesn't mean you shouldn't have employees. It means you need different employees! Hiring the right person for the job is a hard work. I have a rigorous procedure that I use to find, hire, and train employees for my company. And if someone isn't a good fit, I start all over again. I am ruthless with my company because I have to be. I am in charge of the profits and losses and I am the only one that will be this passionate about my company. If employees aren't working out, off they go. I can't afford to keep them if they are sabotaging my efforts.

"Hire slow and fire fast."
- Dan Kennedy

I recently had surgery. After a year of gallbladder attacks, it was time to have my gallbladder removed. During the two weeks of bed rest, my company continued to grow. How? My company is built like a machine. Every part interacts with the other parts to create a living, moving, client-producing machine. Every employee knows his or her job, all the marketing is systemized, and we can continue to grow without me physically "hustling." I have broken down this machine into 5 essential elements and we teach these principles in my coaching program. When you work with me, you'll receive instructions on how you can do the exact same thing in your company!

How to Delegate:

- Write down what you expect (do not expect people to remember verbal instructions.) Have a detailed operation manual with instructions, FAQs, checklists, and procedures clearly spelled out.

- INSPECT what you expect. Check up on them. Regularly, tweak what is incorrect. Use technology to stay informed.

- TRUST them to do a good job. Empower them to make decisions on their own. Praise them when they do!

- Meet with them regularly to discuss what is going well and what needs to be improved upon. Have weekly staff meetings, either in person or on a conference phone line.

- Give them FREEDOM to do a good job without you looking over their shoulder 24/7. When they do well, praise them!

- Tell them you will "zoom in" occasionally and tweak what needs to be changed. By forewarning them, it won't feel like you are micro-managing. They will know this is coming.

- Look at the big picture. Are things running smoothly? What can be fixed or changed?

If you are in the darkness of sickness and chaos, and you have not set up systems, just push through. The light WILL come again. You WILL make it through. When hope has returned, and you have energy once more, set up your systems (or get someone to help you set them up.)

Living in perpetual crisis-mode is not healthy. Yes, crisis happens to all of us. We must expect it, for death and disease do not pass over any of our lives—it touches us somehow, whether directly or through our friends and families. However, if you are always going from one crisis to another, something is wrong. You should not be spending your days putting out fires. If you are, then it's time for an overhaul of your systems, staff, and procedures.

When you have come out of your crisis, do not just push forward. Look backwards—what can you learn from the experience? What systems or people can be put in place so that things do not fall apart the next time life throws you a curve ball?

Take the time to analyze what can be changed and improved upon. Take notes. Write it down. Then implement it.

You CAN make it through the darkness and to the other side.

"If you are going through hell, keep going."

- Winston Churchill

Whatever you are going through, lean on God to be your strength. Surrender to Him and He will guide you through.

In 1989, Anthony Gatto, a professional juggler and record-holder, juggled 5 clubs for 45 minutes and 2 seconds. If he were to add 1 or 2 more clubs, he couldn't juggle more than a minute. Yet, you and I try to juggle 8 or 9 different hats and responsibilities! To juggle motherhood successfully—a job, a house, a family, and friends—we need to be strategic in everything we do.

1. Give momentum to one area at a time

Because I homeschool, I do school with my kids first thing in the morning and I ignore the cleaning and the emails. I give it my complete focus. After lunch, I switch into work mode and at dinnertime; I turn on some music, put on my apron, and switch into just mom-mode. I have staff meetings once a week where I give a lot of effort to my company, and when I'm home, I'm back in mom-mode. My office signifies "work" and the kitchen table is "school."

2. Systematize

I have set up reliable, predictable systems for my company to confidently ensure that when someone finds my company and goes to my website, there is a predictable action that they will take, and my employees will respond to, so they become a new client. It's not accidental that my company continues to grow every single year. I've set up systems to ensure that my website is being found, that clients are requesting more information, and we are providing clear follow-up steps to give them outstanding customer service—even before they have signed up or become our client. I teach all of this in my coaching program. I teach business owners how to systemize their business for predictable growth.

I love to mystery shop my client's businesses. I call the company, pretending to be a prospective client. I record the phone call, and email it to the owner with notes on what can be improved and I provide them with a phone script that guarantees more sales.

I also love to provide website assessments for companies. I get on the phone with business owners, we do a screen share on our computers, and I give them feedback on the layout, the copywriting, the call to action, and the flow. My husband Chris does SEO assessments, to provide the business owner with a report of how the website is ranking online and what can be improved.

You can find out more about our services at www.neveralonecoaching.com.

Early on, I decided that my first priority had to be my children because I only get each of them in my house for 18 years. This forced me to organize, systemize, and automate everything I possibly could in my company and in my home. Because I truly love to work and I love growing my company, I knew I had to be very strategic to do both.

Before I got all my systems set up, there were a couple years when nothing was coming out of my mouth, but inside my head, I was screaming, "I can't do it all!" That was a signal that something had to change. I felt angry for several years and I realized, "Anger is good. It's prompting me to change something." It forced me to evaluate everything and get help.

A couple strategies I learned along the way:

Bundling:

Moms are masters at multi-tasking, but if you're strategic, you can bundle multiple activities so your kids are learning while you are driving or working. When you're working, they don't need screen time the whole time. Kids can entertain themselves and it can be educational. Intentionally fill your home with educational activities. Train your children to entertain themselves and learn on their own. Do not feel obligated to "play" with them all the time. Use screens for a limited time each day, but do not be scared of your children saying, "I'm bored!" because that's when their true creativity is born!

When my kids were preschoolers, I used to have Ikea buckets filled with fun activities stored in the dining room, in cupboards with baby locks. I only took out the busy buckets when I needed the baby, toddler, or preschooler to keep busy when I was homeschooling the older ones or when I needed to get some work done on my computer. I had buttons, Playdoh, counting bears, puzzles, magnets, shapes and letters, and other "messy" activities in the buckets. The preschoolers were thrilled because the buckets were a novelty. I put "messy" activities in those buckets and locked them up so they only came out when I was sitting right there near them. It kept my little ones busy and provided sanity for me!

When you just need a break from all the questions and little voices, you can keep your children learning by utilizing audio books or radio drama stories or learning CDs (we love Adventures in Odyssey and Jonathan Park.) I kept a stash in the kitchen and in the car, and they were lifesavers! You'll keep your kids' brains occupied and you can recharge your own.

Outsourcing:

You may choose to host teenagers at your house for a party, or lead a Bible study for your church because these things are important to you, but choose to pay someone to mow the lawn, shovel the snow, balance your books, or answer your company's phones. Outsourcing is a powerful tool to off-load responsibilities to free up time and energy for the areas you care most about. You really, truly can't do it all, so choose what you really want to do and outsource the rest.

When my kids were very young, I had to hire a babysitter one day a week and work very hard in limited, concentrated hours so I could work uninterrupted. Do you know how much time people waste when they work full time? They know they have all week, so they waste time, mess around, and push things off to the next day. Honestly, you have the ability to be more effective and get more done in eight hours than most people do in 40. Just be focused, disciplined, and determined, and you can accomplish anything! Do not think that you have to work full time to make your company grow! You need to be strategic and purposeful—not tied to your desk for 40 hours per week.

When my husband was working full time and gone 7:45 am to 6:30 pm and I had 4 kids under the age of seven, I used a grocery delivery service. When the man brought my groceries into my kitchen and unloaded them onto my kitchen table, I ALMOST hugged him (I think he would have understood). More expensive, yes, and I had to stretch the food, but it was WORTH IT during that season of life. There was no way I could take 4 kids to the store by myself—it would have wasted my time and zapped my sanity. Are you being smart with your time? If you're stressed out all the time, stop and re-evaluate what you are doing and what you are pushing through. Start questioning everything you're doing and ask yourself, "Is there a better way to do this?" There probably is!

Tech-flex: You can use technology to stay in touch with everything you are juggling, and not be stuck behind a desk or in an office. I can run my kids to and from activities; check on my security cameras at the studio, check my email, etc, even when I'm not at my studio. It doesn't mean I work MORE, it means I use technology to be flexible to work from wherever I want. We have the great gift of technology. Use it wisely and don't be sucked into games, Facebook, or Netflix. Let technology serve you and help you streamline your processes.

3. Communicate Schedules and Expectations

I am very strategic with my kids and my calendar. To keep everything running smoothly, my husband needs to know the plan for the week, and so do my kids. If you join my coaching program, we will talk more about this, but here's the big picture:

Every Sunday night, I write out our family's schedule on a white board, so my kids can see what is coming up and what they're doing for the week. I also synchronize my paper calendar to our family Google calendar, so my husband knows exactly what's coming up. (Someone commented to me: "That sounds like a lot of work!" Yes, it is. But it's completely worth it because it makes our whole week run more smoothly!)

Every Sunday night, I rewrite my To-Do list for the week, so I know what to focus on for the upcoming week. I want to hit the ground running on Monday morning and not waste the day trying to figure out my goals and focus. On Sunday night, I'm rested and I think clearly. It's a perfect time to set these goals. I don't dread Mondays. I wake up excited and ready to tackle the week! (If you hate Mondays, you need to make a change in your life. It's possible to make strategic changes to love your life again!)

Every Saturday, I pull out a laminated chore list to get the house completely clean and restocked for the week. I've divided up the chores so all the kids know what they are doing. They check them off throughout the morning so I know what got done (change the litter box, do the laundry, clean out the cars, restock bathrooms with toilet paper, refill the paper towels in the kitchen, etc.) Chore day sets us up for a wonderful week because we aren't distracted by these tasks throughout the week. You don't need distractions. You need clear focus to grow your company!

Every day, kids refer to the job list on the side of the fridge, so they know who is helping with dishes and cleaning the countertops. When my kids were little and couldn't read yet, I used picture charts for them to know what jobs they needed to do. Don't get sucked into Pinterest and making this perfect! Just get it done fast so your kids can understand.

As my kids have gotten older, we've switched from picture charts to lists and they are responsible for reading what jobs and tasks they need to do, and for looking at the calendar to see what is happening for the day. They often remind me when it's time to walk out the door for an activity! I love that they are learning responsibility because I'm a busy work-at-home mom.

When they were little, my kids used to whine: "What are we DOING today?" and it wasn't necessarily because they were bored, but because they needed to know what to expect. I wrote a schedule for school, meals, snacks, and screen time, and told them they could play Legos, play outside, build a fort, read a book, or do whatever else they wanted to the rest of the time. I called this a "Normal Day" so when nothing exciting was planned, I could declare, "Today is a Normal Day!" and they knew what that meant.

Think Ahead

Most people are rushing around, putting out fires, responding to whatever need comes up. If you want to run a successful business and raise your kids, you cannot live like this. You have to be thinking ahead always. What's coming next? You have to be one or two steps ahead at all time. (Read the book, *Margin*.) Allow extra time for everything. If you need to leave the house at 3:00 to arrive for a 3:30 activity, start leaving the house 15 minutes earlier, at 2:45! My kids are always losing one dance shoe or one soccer cleat. When I build in 15 minutes of "leaving time," we can search for the missing piano book or grab that water bottle. It's still chaotic, but we arrive on time to the activities!

One tip that a friend told me has really helped. She told me that she divides her day into 3 parts: morning, afternoon, and evening. She only fills one or two sections per day. So, if we have a morning activity, we are home in the afternoon. We may leave again in the evening, but we try not to be gone all day. This has built margin into our lives and we don't feel frantic and crazy all the time.

"If you want something you've never had, you must be willing to do what you've never done!"
-Thomas Jefferson

More ways to keep your sanity

Pamper yourself: Buy new pillows, sheets, and a comforter. Buy new towels. These small things will make you thankful for your life and your home. You don't need a new home—you can upgrade what you have and feel like things are new!

Take a vacation: Most people don't go on vacation because it's "so expensive." We have found creative ways to travel because we love traveling! You don't have to fly, get a hotel and rent a car! Choose one of those. We have driven to vacation destinations and stayed in a hotel (don't drive too far when your kids are small! Stay local! You'll save your sanity and they will be excited about going just an hour away!) Or we have chosen to fly, but then we stayed with friends and used their car. We have also used a relative's unused rental property or time-share to save money (many people have a time-share they aren't using and they feel guilty about it so they would be happy to give you a good deal on it!) If you're creative, you can get away from normal life, get refreshed, and not spend a ton of money! When your business is systemized and automated, you can step away and things will continue to run smoothly!

Set goals: I am a visionary and an activator. I like to take quick action and take risks. However, I have learned that my vision and action are not directly related. They are several steps apart. So I have to see the big vision in the distance, but take small action steps to get on my way. As much as I would like to take giant strides toward my goal, growth is sustained and possible when I start small and build layer upon layer. I didn't grow from 100 music students to 400 students in a year. Even though 500 students is my goal, I have to make small changes and grow by 10 students per month. That seems so small! But multiplied times 12 months, I can grow 120 students per year! I also have to figure out steps forward and steps backward. I might enroll 50 students in a month, but 30 drop out, quit, or take a break. As long as I am moving forward, that's all that matters. I figure out what I can do to stop the losses, but I also keep focusing on getting new students.

When I wanted to move out of our tiny rambler into a bigger house, I obsessively looked online at houses for sale. I drove around, checking out neighborhoods. I prayed like crazy. Chris told me over and over, "We can't move. We can't sell this house. It will never work." I kept dreaming, praying, and brainstorming solutions.

One day I had a great idea. What if we didn't sell our house, but rented it out instead? And what if we didn't buy a new house, but we rented one instead? It was unconventional, but Chris agreed it could work (Chris agreed to my crazy plan! Major miracle right there!)

I went on my computer and looked for houses for rent. Unbelievably, I only found two houses that worked for our family and one of them is the one we moved into! The whole process took only 2 months. I don't think I could recreate that process if I tried. It all happened because of vision, determination, and prayer. The timing was right and God made it happen. Not all your dreams will come true so quickly. In reality, my dream didn't come true quickly, either. It had been 2 years of wanting to move, looking at houses, praying, and crying. When the time was right, God said: "Now." We listened and obeyed, and ended up in a beautiful house with 3 acres.

You have to look ahead and know where you're going! Don't keep those dreams in your head. Make a list. Put it where you can see it. Think about those goals every day. Make a vision board so you can SEE where you're headed. One year I made a board and decided I wanted to take my kids to Chicago and Washington DC on an Amtrak train. I wanted to go to Cozumel with Chris' parents. I wanted to grow my business to a specific number of students and I wanted to finish my first book. I did ALL of those things that year, thanks to my vision board. Before I create a vision board, I think and I pray about my goals. I choose some goals that are attainable and some that are out of reach. I talk to my husband and show my kids. I include some motivational quotes like, "Do it scared" and "If your dreams don't scare you, they aren't big enough!" and "Do what you can, with what you have, where you are."

Keep a smile file: When someone gives you a birthday card or a thank you note, keep those cards in a file where you can look back and get encouragement when you need it. Where you're chasing your dreams and working hard, discouragement is always just around the corner. When I'm in the thick of hard business decisions and pushing hard to accomplish my goals, I tend to forget that people even like me! I start second guessing everything. Then, I flip through cards and notes and I remember that people appreciate me. They love me. They believe in me. And it gives me momentum to keep going.

Download the companion workbook to this book at
www.neveralonecoaching.com. You'll break down your
schedule and learn how to simplify and automate your
processes and procedures.

CHAPTER 5

Love what you do.
Do what you love.

"Nobody can go back and start a new beginning, but anyone can start today and make a new ending."
–Maria Robinson

If I had one message for the world, it would be: "Do what you love and love what you do!" God wired you for a specific mission on this earth. No one else is exactly like you. You have unique gifts, abilities, and talents. Your personality is one-of-a-kind.

Life is short... so you must do more of what makes you come alive! If you don't know what that is, then start trying lots of different things! Try until you find it. If you love to paint, paint! If you love to dance, dance! If you love numbers, work with numbers! If you love to run, go run! If you love music, please make music!

Have you ever had headphones on, listening to your favorite song, and you just feel swept away into the music? Maybe you're taking a brisk walk around a beautiful lake, with the sunlight glimmering off the gentle waves of the water. Your soul literally starts to sing with the music. You resonate with the words, and you can't hear anything else. Nothing else is clamoring for your attention. You're just surrounded by the music. You are swept away in the melody, the harmonies, and the catchy riffs. When you are surrounded by your life's purpose and when you are fully engaged in the things that you love, that you are good at, that God has placed inside of you, your soul will sing every day.

In the book, *Unique Ability*, the author explains that when you take two of your skills or talents and put them together, you create Unique Ability. You are able to do something that makes others say "Wow! How do you do that?" Growing up, I was always very musical. I won awards in competitions for singing, I was chosen for select choirs, I accompanied soloists and the choir on the piano, and I had lead singing roles in theatre. Seemingly separate, I was also always a leader. I became the captain of the cheerleading squad, I led Bible Studies, I always won prizes for selling the most candy bars or magazines for school fundraisers, and I was producing newsletters at an embarrassingly young age. When I went off to college, I struggled with what to major in. Music or Journalism? I loved both writing and music. I chose music, but God has used my love for writing in a million ways. And most importantly, my love for sales and business combined with both music and writing has created a dynamic explosion that has resulted in a company that grosses over a half million dollars per year. Just my love of music would not have grown my company. Just my love of writing would not have advanced my school of music or my coaching business. And my love of business without a love for people and education would not have grown my music school. My Unique Ability explosion has been the combination of business, music, education, people, writing, and teaching. Now, I would not be where I am today if I decided to "work on my weaknesses" and really get better at bookkeeping because I'm not so great at that. No way. God has called us to use our strengths and abilities for His glory—not try to focus on our weaknesses! My husband loves numbers and says bookkeeping is "easy." Okay, whatever man. You do your strengths and I'll do mine!

When Chris focuses on what gives him energy, he's not exhausted and drained. He does bookkeeping and numbers for many companies and he breezes through it because it's easy for him! I want to lie on the floor and cry.

Conversely, if Chris has to be creative and write copy for a newsletter or email, he gets frustrated and worked up. I can crank out words effortlessly. So why wouldn't I do what comes easily to me and let him stick to what is easy for him?

It's simple. Do what you love and what you are good at. Outsource or delegate the things you hate or that make you angry. At the beginning of building my company, I pushed through things that were really hard for me. I had to. Chris wasn't home and I couldn't afford to hire anyone to help me. But after the foundation of my business was laid, I was able to take the list of "Things I hate to do" and hire staff and services to take care of those things for me. Sometimes I'm tempted to pick tasks that I don't like to do back up, just because it's easier than explaining to someone else how I want them done. But, inevitably, I get irritated and frustrated. My energy gets drained. It takes discipline to stay within my strengths so I can gain energy from those activities and really stay in my Unique Ability zone.

Remember when you were five years old? What did you love then? Before the world told you to grow up, before anyone told you "it's impossible," what did you love to do?

We come into this world hard-wired with our mission, our calling, our purpose. You just have to figure out what it is.

> *"Never give up on what you really want to do. The person with big dreams is more powerful than one with all the facts."*
> *- H. Jackson Brown Jr.*

In your business, what is the part that you absolutely love? What are the parts you endure or don't enjoy at all?

A couple years ago, I went on a mission to figure out who I am, how I'm wired, and what God created me to do. I started a note on Evernote and started listing times in my business that I absolutely loved. I listed what I couldn't stand to do. The areas that I absolutely can't stand to do, or drain my energy quickly is what I have now delegated to other staff members (or my husband.) The things I love to do give me energy, so not only do I enjoy those parts of my work, but I also actually get more accomplished because I'm so energized (and not drained) from what I'm doing.

I also took several personality assessments and listed the results. I studied the words to figure out WHO I am and how I am wired. I highly recommend you do this, too! On my website, you can download a workbook companion to this book. You'll find out how YOU are wired and what you should be focusing on in your business. Find it at www.neveralonecoaching.com.

I talk to people that don't know how they are wired, they don't know their purpose, and they can't figure out their Unique Ability. Here's why: you're too close to it. Pay attention to when someone says, "Wow! How did you do that?" and you reply, "It was easy!" That is a clue to your wiring and gifts. We overlook what comes easily and naturally to us because it's just too easy! We assume it's easy for everyone else. Not so, my friend. Start your own journal of what you love to do, what is easy for you; And conversely, what you hate, and what frustrates you. Pay attention instead of just pushing through. Stop, notice, and take note. These will be the clues to a successful (and happy) future.

As a mom, I am very intentional about noticing and naming what my kids are good at. My youngest cuts and tapes paper to make 3D models of houses and hot air balloons. It's amazing! My other daughter has endless patience and loves to decorate cupcakes. I would much rather make brownies, throw them in a pan and call it a day. She is wired for details and art, and I always let her know God has created her that way. My second son is both artistic and a whiz at electronics. I always tell him ideas of how those two skills put together will be beneficial in video editing, graphic design, sound engineering, etc. We have to help our kids see what they are naturally good at and stop insisting that they spend all their time improving their weaknesses.

Looking back, my favorite classes in school included writing. But what was most of my time spent on? Improving my math skills. Stupid flash cards. Playing "games" with math. Ugh. Honestly, the entire math thing didn't make sense to me until I grew and matured, and my brain could handle those concepts. Instead of shoving more math down my throat, I wish my teachers and parents had said, "You are really good at writing! It comes naturally to you. Let's do more writing. Let's get you in a creative writing class." I would have been thrilled and it would have prepped me for my future so much more than continuing to try to make math make sense.

Honestly, I am not a proponent of a "well-rounded" education. When I hire people, I hire them for their strengths, not their ability to be somewhat good at everything. I would much rather help my kids get better at what they already love than deprive them in those areas so we can work on their weaknesses.

I encourage you to write a list of your child's natural abilities. Check out the book, *How Am I Smart?* to break down the categories and understand how God has wired your child. Then, be intentional about telling your child what they are good at. Every Valentine's Day, I give each of my kids a construction paper heart with their name listed on top. I write: "You Are..." and then I list out everything I see in them, including skills and character qualities. I want these words burned in their mind and heart. I think it's easier as a parent to see what my kids are naturally good at and the activities that they love and are wired for, than it is to see in myself. That's because the world has forced us to grow up and get practical. But the world is wrong! We need to stay in our strengths and bring to our companies our unique skills, gifts, talents, and personality. You'll be happier and your company will grow and flourish!

I don't love cleaning, so I hire a house cleaner. I don't love numbers, so my husband does all the Profit and Loss statements and bookkeeping. I like to do the layout for my newsletter, but it frustrates me and takes my husband a fraction of the time to get it done, so now he does it for me. I like to work the front desk at my studio, but I'd rather be home with my kids, so I hire receptionists to work for me. I don't like gardening (I thought I did. I tried it, but three years later it was dying from lack of attention and I realized I loved doing other things much more,) so we sodded over our garden so I wouldn't feel guilty every time I looked out the window. I've experienced a huge transformation in my life since I've intentionally started focusing on my strengths and doing what I love to do. I'm happier, my kids are happier, and my company is flourishing and growing.

Five years ago, I very intentionally asked myself, "What do I truly want out of life?" The answer was to grow my company, homeschool, enjoy my children, and to travel with them. And that's what we are doing now! I re-defined my goals, I eliminated time-wasters, I automated my home and business to run like a well-oiled machine, and now I get to love my life and my business! I'm happy and fulfilled, and you can be too!

Chapter 6

How working from home and homeschooling work together

"Most of the important things in the world have been accomplished by people who have kept on trying when there seemed to be no hope at all."
-Dale Carnegie

People ask me all the time, "How do you homeschool and run a business?" But the truth is that they go hand in hand. The best business advice from all expert coaches is to leverage your business, multiply yourself, become a manager of people, and step back so your company can run smoothly without your 24/7 involvement. By choosing to homeschool, and making that a priority for our family, it's simply impossible for me to run my company 24/7. By committing to my children's education, I had to figure out how to systemize, automate, and delegate. On the other side, homeschooling experts will all agree: "Homeschooling is not like school at home." They recommend simplifying, letting children play, going at the child's pace, letting curiosity lead the way, and limiting the actual "school" time at the kitchen table with workbooks. The truth is—real learning comes from real life. True understanding occurs when I am really curious about the subject. So working from home part time has actually forced me to be a better homeschool mom! I work with the kids one-on-one, I track their progress, I know what they need, but we are done at noon. They have a lot of time for self-directed, curiosity-based learning time. They listen to audio books, pretend, invent, experiment, and branch off into extracurricular activities such as theatre, baseball, dance, horseback riding, art, and playing musical instruments. They have time to figure out Minecraft; they write stories on the computer; they build forts, and they get to be just kids. It's easy for me to "let go" and not micromanage because I am working! As an added bonus, they see what it's like to run a company, interview prospective employees, schedule meetings, deal with emergencies, and celebrate victories. My 15-year-old son said, "Sure, you could just homeschool me, but then I wouldn't see what it's really like to run a company. I'm getting the best education by just watching you." Many of my friends own companies and homeschool, and as their kids get older and enter college; their kids will actually work in the family business. What an advantage! Their children are gaining real life experience and training that will put them head and shoulders above their peers. I want that for my kids. I want them to have real experience before they go out into the world.

I interview young college graduates all the time, and they may have a degree, but if they have zero experience, I can't hire them. It's always disastrous. Conversely, the ones who volunteered or worked through high school and college have a huge advantage. They've already been in the trenches and they already have a baseline knowledge about what the job entails. Parents; give your kids real life experience outside of the classroom! And start young! My oldest has volunteered for VBS, kids church, preschool classes, theatre classes, and has been a junior counselor. He has mowed lawns, hauled theatre sets, chopped wood, and learned about landscaping. He needs these skill and tool for life! We can do English, handwriting, history, science and math, but these real-life experiences are what will really prepare him for life.

Benefits of homeschooling and working

1. Freedom and Control

When people ask me why I homeschool, I tell them I love the freedom and control. And yes, owning a business and homeschooling is a ton of responsibility, but I love the freedom of both!

When things are stressful and employees have quit, I can focus more time on work. When things are running smoothly, I spend more concentrated time with my kids, traveling, going to museums, being outside, and visiting friends.

2. Lifestyle

I am modeling a lifestyle for my kids. My balancing, juggling, outsourcing, delegating, and automating is teaching them how to live life in a balanced way. I am very conscious that I am mentoring my kids—through life, I am teaching them, observing them, and training them for their future.

I love to follow the seasons. I work a lot in the winter and get a lot of school done when the weather is cold and yucky. When the weather is beautiful in the spring and fall, we drop everything and go to the apple orchard or to the park for a picnic. I sign my kids up for many summer camps in the summer to keep them busy and active (and so I can work!)

When my kids became teenagers, I realized that I needed to be intentional with my time with them and not just available because we are in the same house. I intentionally schedule one-on-one dates with each kid (ideally once per month.) We go out to coffee or have lunch together. I mostly just listen and let them know that I'm here for them. If they want to talk about Minecraft or superheroes the whole time, I listen. If I listen to the small things now, they'll trust me with the big stuff later.

"Listen earnestly to anything your children want to tell you, no matter what. If you don't listen eagerly to the little stuff when they are little, they won't tell you the big stuff when they are big because to them all of it has always been big stuff."
– Catherine M. Wallace

Every Monday morning, I have "Mentor Meetings" with each of my kids. We talk about the schedule for the week, what they need from me (a permission slip signed, a birthday gift, new shoes,) and we talk about the projects they are working on. I ask them what is going well and what we can change. I ask them what books they are reading. They all look forward to mentor meetings and remind me about them if I ever forget!

The best part of working from home is being available to my kids. Even if I'm working, they know where to find me and they know they can always ask to talk. Now that I have teenagers in the house, when they need to talk, I drop everything. They are facing big decisions and dilemmas that affect their future and I'm so thankful that I can be there when they need me. I know babies and toddlers are demanding, but the whole game changes with teenagers. The stakes are higher. The mistakes are bigger. We still need to be available for our kids as they grow—just in a different way.

3. True Apprenticeship

I am keenly aware that I am providing my kids with an internship in my home. I am intentionally training them on all the skills I know about: business, customer service, finances, marketing, websites, video editing, picture editing, etc. Whatever you are good at, pass it on to your kids! Woodworking, gardening, cooking, painting, finances—whatever it is, be intentional and pass along real life skills to your kids!

Chapter 7

Let's Talk Business.

"A ship in port is safe, but that's not what ships are built for."
-Rear Admiral Grace Murray Hopper

Imagine that you are running a lemonade stand. You bought all the equipment: you have the water, the sugar, the lemons, the cups, and a pitcher. You made a beautiful sign, you have a cashbox, and you're open for business. You are running your own social media, so you post on Facebook: "Lemonade! $1.00!" You tweet out cute sayings every hour and you write a blog all about your passion for lemonade. Then you wait. You aren't getting as many customers as you would like, so you create a business Page on Facebook and post on there. You're trying hard to get a lot of likes for your page while researching the best way to boost a post. You blog some more. A couple of customers drive by and purchase the lemonade. They love it. You make more lemonade and keep up the advertising. One customer mentions that they stumbled upon you on accident and they would have found you sooner if you had some better signage on the main road. You thank them for the advice and then consider buying some yard signs to have more signage on main intersections. The thoughts that run through your head are: "I've barely made a profit! After buying the initial supplies and then selling some product today, I've barely made any money. And now, I'm supposed to go spend more money on signage? But, if I don't buy more signage, how will more people find me?"

You have two choices. You can sit and wait, and keep all your profit, or you can invest in more advertising to get more customers to sell even more lemonade.

You hear your baby crying in the baby monitor. Oh, no. The baby woke up sooner than you expected. Now what? Close up the lemonade stand until naptime tomorrow? Keep the baby on your lap while you keep the stand open? You decide to stay open and the baby can enjoy the sunshine and play near you. This works until you've run out of lemons. You need to go purchase more supplies. Now what? Close up the stand to go to the store? Order on Amazon (and wait two days?) Hire someone to go to the store for you? Or hire someone to sit at the stand while you go to the store?

The small-minded lemonade stand owner will close up the shop, pack up the baby, go to the store, and only buy cups and lemons with a coupon. She won't buy yard signs because they are "too expensive" and she'll continue to use just social media marketing. She'll juggle the baby and the lemonade stand, have limited hours (because the baby needs her and she needs to make dinner,) and she'll make a small profit. It's fun to run the stand, but she is exhausted. It's a lot of work doing all the advertising on social media, blogging every day, running to the store for more supplies, and taking care of the baby.

The smart business owner of the lemonade stand will realize she has a good thing going here. People love the lemonade, but most people don't know where she is located. She decides to hire someone to sell lemonade for her so she can order yard signs, put them up on every major intersection, shop for more supplies, and go introduce herself to other business owners in the area. She meets quite a few people and they agree to spread the word that lemonade is for sale just around the corner. She is tired of running to the store for new supplies all the time, so she orders them on auto-ship, directly to her home. It's still a lot of work to manage her new employee and all the ordering and inventory of supplies. But it's nice to be inside in the air conditioning during the hottest part of the day. When the baby wakes up, she can give her full attention to her child, and she knows that if the business needs her attention, she'll get a phone call or an email. The new signage and supplies are expensive. It takes a couple weeks of all the profits going straight back into the business, but she has never had to take out a loan. This is the first week that she has made a profit and she is thrilled! Business is steady. She decides to extend her hours and hire more help. The new employees are amazing. Not only do they make lemonade and sell it, they clean the stand and always keep things looking nice. They are friendly and customers love their big smiles. The smart business owner has time to think of new ideas. She decides to roll out a new flavor: strawberry lemonade! She makes new yard signs, posts it on social media, and even gets interviewed by the local paper. When the baby wakes up, they take a walk to the park. She pushes the baby on the swings, glances down at her phone and the notification says the strawberry lemonade is a hit. They've had their biggest day of revenue to date! She calls her husband and says, "Let's go out to dinner tonight."

Here's how you know you have a business: You've identified a need and you've filled it. You have a solution to a problem, and people are willing to pay you for that solution. You are making money! That's the definition of a business.

When you are the only one in your business doing all the work, you are a technician. When you multiply yourself and you hire more technicians, a receptionist, or an administrative assistant, you are able to focus on what only you can do or what you do best. When you hire a bookkeeper because you hate details and numbers, you are freeing up brain space to focus on your creative business. When you are a baker, and you rent an industrial space (instead of continuing to cook in your kitchen,) you are multiplying your efforts by having multiple ovens and large equipment to make your cookies in larger quantities. When you are a general contractor, and you start hiring sub-contractors, you can build a house much faster than when you were doing all the work yourself.

I had a friend who was selling handmade signs. She came to me, frustrated that she was working all the time and she had a lot of orders, but it seemed like she wasn't making any money. So we had a "Money Talk."

I asked her: "How much do you charge for your signs?"

"Forty dollars," she replied.

"Okay. How many hours does it take you to make each sign?"

"Well," she said, "because I custom design each one, let's see. I have to make the design, send the proof to the customer, set my machine to print, and then I have to sand and stain the wood and apply the vinyl lettering. I would say about 5 hours per sign."

I held back my gagging. "So, Anna," I said, "You spend 5 hours making one sign that you sell for $40. That's $8 per hour that you're making."

"No," she said, "It's less than that because the wood and the vinyl lettering cost about $5 per sign."

"Ok," I readjusted my math. "Take $5 off the $40. That's $35. Divide that by 5 hours and you're making $7 per hour."

"I never thought about it that way before," she said, sadness in her eyes.

"Here's what you can do," I advised. "Start making your signs in bulk. Spend a couple hours staining a lot of the wood. Then, when you make vinyl lettering, make a lot at one time. Don't just make one sign—make 10. Then you'll have inventory ready to sell and you won't have to work on just one sign at a time."

"I can't do that," she said. "My customers come to me because they are hand-made, custom designs. They love picking out the color and the design. They often customize the words and will choose to have their last name and the year of their marriage on the sign."

"That's wonderful!" was my response. "So, now you need to charge more for the sign. I would start at $110 per custom sign."

"Oh, no. I could never do that," Anna said. "My customers love my prices. I think $40 is steep! I could never charge more."

I sat back in my chair, crossed my arms, and said: "Anna, you can't have it both ways. You can't have a low cost, highly customized product. You'll never make any money. That's why you are frustrated. Your signs are beautiful, but if you have to spend all day making one and you only make $35, it's just not worth it. You either have to raise your prices or you have to duplicate your product and stop customizing everything."

Anna looked at me and said: "I have another side business."

"You do? What is it?" I asked, surprised.

"I'm a face painter. I'm really good. I've studied multiple designs and been practicing on my kids. I do full color art on kids' faces and the result is stunning. I charge $50 per hour and I travel to kids' birthday parties. I can usually make $100-$200 in a day. I schedule the parties on the weekend when my husband is home and so I don't have to pay for childcare."

"Anna!" I said. "That's it! That's the business you should be focusing on!" We looked at her website and I gave her an assessment of what should be changed. We worked on her call to action and made the website client-focused. Then, we went "under the hood" of her website and fixed her SEO. A couple weeks later, Anna called me.

"Jen! You won't believe it! People are calling me about face painting almost every day! I used to get only new clients from referrals and by word of mouth, but now people are finding me online! They said my website is bright, fun, and easy to understand. They are booking me as a face painter, Jen!" Her excitement and enthusiasm made me laugh out loud. I was thrilled for her!

Today, Anna still does face painting. She has quit advertising her handmade signs, although I'm sure she still makes them for fun or for gifts. It took an assessment with me, a business coach, for her to see the holes in her business, where she was headed, and how she could adjust her path. Now, she's working less but making more money.

She loves what she does, but she has time for gardening, homeschooling, and even dancing. She picked a venue for her skills and her passion for painting and directed it in an industry that people understand, want, and are looking for. Events are always more fun with face painting! Anna will always have a demand for what she does and she can say "yes" or "no" to opportunities as they come along, based on her life and priorities. It's win-win.

"Fall down seven times, get up eight."
Japanese Proverb

A couple years ago, my daughter was taking a gymnastics class. One particular night stands out very vividly in my mind.

The gym was sweaty and humid. The girls were working hard on the bars, beam, and vault. But my attention was really drawn to the girls on the floor. They ranged from age 8 to 14 and they were doing flips and twists—tricks I usually see on TV at the Olympics.

However, not one of them was landing on their feet.

Yet, the coaches were yelling: "Good one! Great job! YES!"

I stood mesmerized, forgetting my own daughter on the beam, in her beginner class. The teen girls were sweating, hearts pounding, hair mussed, chests heaving. Again and again, they got back in line, ran, vaulted into the air to attempt the trick again. Beautiful twists and turns— sometimes aided by an extra lift by their coach.

Bam. Bam. Bam. They all fell squarely on their behinds. Push up, stand up, and try again. Coaches bellowing: "Yes! Like that! Do it again!"

I couldn't tear my eyes away. The power of coaching— encouragement, coaxing, prodding, and leading— it was influencing me on a deeper level than just gymnastics.

There was a time in my business when I felt 100% alone with my questions and searching. I didn't know how to grow, I didn't know how to manage the day-to-day operations of my studio, and I didn't know where to go for help.

I literally would Google search music studio after music studio around the country, trying desperately to "peer" in the windows of their company for a hint or clue on how to run this thing.

In July of 2011, my Google search led me to a business coach who specialized in helping music schools. It is absolutely no accident why we've grown from 70 students to over 400 in only 5 years. It is 100% due to coaching that I've received by my mentors. "You can do this! Yes! Try again! That's the way!" And sometimes he says, "No. Focus. Don't get distracted."

A couple years ago, I was teaching a piano lesson to a classy lady that I taught for over 10 years. Recently, she had taken about 18 months off. When she came back, she gave me a huge hug, but I could tell she was nervous about playing piano again. She opened a book that was way beneath her playing ability and she insisted we start with something simple. I obliged her wishes, but then I turned to a harder song, closer to the place where she left off. She looked anxiously at me and then proceeded to try just the right hand. I nodded. "Now, the left hand," I said. She did.

"Now," I said, "Put the hands together. You can do this."
She laughed nervously and said, "You think so? Oh, Jen,
you always believe in me more than I believe in myself."

And she did it! It wasn't perfect, but she played the song! I
beamed. She beamed. It was an awesome moment.

What struck me the most while watching the advanced
gymnastics team was how often the girls fell. You see, while
you are perfecting a new trick or skill, it's not about
sticking every landing. It's not about being perfect. It's
about getting out there and trying. It's about sweat and
tears, and about trying over and over and over again. It's
about perfecting technique and gaining more height every
time you try.

My daughter loved gymnastics, but during a busy season of
our lives, she took about 5 months off. She had been trying
desperately to do a cartwheel on the beam without falling
off. And you know what? When she came back, she wasn't
weaker—she was mentally stronger, a little older, and more
determined. Within a few weeks of being back, she
mastered that skill! When I see her do a cartwheel on the

beam, I'm inspired. She may have needed a break, but she never quit. She kept trying.

As our businesses continue to grow, we run into new problems and we face new challenges. But one thing is for sure: with the help of a coach, we will always have support and we will always be moving forward to the next level!

How You Can Have a Coach in Your Life

1. Lean on lifelong friends who know where you've been, where you are, and where you're going. Make sure your friends bring positive influences, and not pulling you down with negativity. You truly have to guard your heart and only choose friendships that will encourage you along your journey. Stay close to friends who have known you a long time and who understand your dreams and goals. Work hard to find new friends who are on the same journey as you are. Being an entrepreneur or a work-at-home mom can be a lonely life. You can feel like you are crazy or you're the only one who chooses to live like this. Join Facebook groups or networking groups and regularly interact with people who "get" you.

2. Sign up for lessons or a class. Push yourself to learn more, grow, and take on a challenge. This doesn't necessarily mean going back to college! You can learn at your own pace versus having an intense college schedule thrust upon your family. There are so many online classes and programs available that are easy to insert into your life and won't put a strain on your family time, and yet you will learn valuable, cutting-edge information that will improve your business! Never stop asking questions, getting curious, and learning how to run your business better. (Bonus: you are modeling a life-long learning for your kids!)

3. Hire a professional business coach or life coach. I have spent thousands of dollars per year on business coaching. My entire business turned around and quadrupled in size because I found a business coach. These results have caused me to work with several different coaches because I learn different things from every single one. The people I've met along the way have been one of the best parts! We are doing this life together and we truly understand the journey.

You can join my coaching program and meet moms just like you—that are working and raising kids. You'll get direct access to me and my techy husband and you can ask questions about your life and your business. Every month, we tackle a new topic and we'll help you achieve real growth and success in your company and at home!

"Life's a marathon, not a sprint."
- Phillip C. McGraw

This crazy life we are living is a marathon, not a sprint. You have to pace yourself, have people around you to cheer you on, and have coaches pushing you to keep going!

When he was in 8th grade, my oldest son ran cross-country. It was the first year a group of homeschoolers had formed a team. I thought for sure we would be the underdogs in comparison to our public school competitors. I cringed as I arrived at our first meet. Surely, our scraggly, inexperienced team would embarrass us. Instead, I was blown away by the entire experience. Parents lined the path and as each student ran past, parents yelled: "You can do it! Keep going! You're almost there!" Coaches ran to various parts of the path and strategically placed themselves at inclines and curves. They were there waiting, a familiar and encouraging voice in the ear of the straining runner. Students not running cheered on their teammates from the sideline. It was so incredibly powerful and moving. Cross-country running is an individual sport and a team sport because the scores count both as a team and for the individual. Not only was our team not the underdog, we had team members who consistently won 1st place ribbons! The student who was consistently last never gave up. He always kept running and sometimes his dad ran alongside him during the final stretch, urging him to "KEEP GOING!"

The entire time I watched the cross-country meets, I could only think about the parallel to real life. Life is hard and exhausting. We have to pace ourselves. And we have to have coaches and teammates cheering us on at different checkpoints. In life, sometimes you walk, sometimes you run. But you keep going. You don't quit.

"Never Give Up!

Never, never, never, never give up.

Never!"

-Winston Churchill

You need to run your own race and not compare yourself to those around you. In cross-country, students are trying to improve their own time and beat their last score. I encourage you to run your own race. Stop comparing yourself to a girlfriend that you think has it all together. She doesn't. Trust me. We all struggle. We all strain under the weight of life. But we can have encouragement and coaching. We can surround ourselves with others who cheer us on. You don't have to run alone.

"Comparison is the death of true self-contentment."

-John Powell

If you work with us, together:

1. We will re-define what you want your life and business to look like.

2. We will eliminate time-wasters and the things that are sucking the life out of your soul.

3. We'll help you set up systems to automate processes in both your home life and business.

4. You'll love what you do in your business again and you'll only do the parts you love.

It's easy to get started. First, like my page on Facebook for daily encouragement. www.facebook.com/jenhickle1. Then, visit my website where you can purchase the companion workbook to this book, www.neveralonecoaching.com. Step by step, you can work through the material to see big changes in your life and in your business! Next, sign up for my coaching program. I can't wait to meet you and help you grow your business!

Made in the USA
San Bernardino, CA
27 August 2016